Save Our Democracy

Save Our Democracy

★★★★★★★

Wake Up Your Unwoke, Undecided, Apolitical, Non-Voting, I-Don't-Care-About-Politics Friends & Family

SAKADA

GeniusWork Publishing

Editors: Elgee Tavanlar Amato and Gayle Sato
Book Cover and Interior Design: Susan Shankin

Published by GeniusWork Publishing, Los Angeles, CA
www.geniusworkpublishing.com

Library of Congress Control Number: 2019919396

ISBN Print: 978-1-7342988-8-8
ISBN Ebook: 978-1-7342988-9-5

Printed in the United States of America

Dedication

To all the activists
who have stayed
vigilant and active
since the 2016 election,
and are working hard
to save our democracy.
Bless you all!

Contents

INTRO-DUC-TION

CALL TO ACTION: SAVE OUR DEMOCRACY

» Focus on waking up **your unwoke friends and family.**

» Talk to them **over the fence** using well-framed conversations.

» Create a tidal wave of Democratic voters in 2020, and **Make America Democratic Again**.

THIS BOOK WILL GUIDE you through these steps, and your friends and family will be grateful that you woke them up before we lost our democracy.

THE FENCES THAT DIVIDE US

The fences are not the strict divisions between Democrats and Republicans, although this book is advocating for the widespread election of Democrats in 2020.

The fences are dividing those who are going to save our Democracy, and those who are enabling its downfall, either actively (Trump-Supporting Republicans) or through their neutrality (Unwoke Voters).

As a society, we need to start talking to each other *over the fence*, before the fences become walls. The divides in America have been cleaved open by the Trumplicans, and it looks like Trump's campaign strategy is to continue to hammer at these divides.

With a simple gesture, each of us can fight this force of division. We can reach out and talk *over the fence*. If this can be successful in neighborhoods, it can be successful in our nation.

It is also important to acknowledge that there are more and more woke Republicans standing up to this administration, and we want to encourage them.

OUR DEMOCRACY IS IN DANGER

In the summer before the 2016 election, I saw the musical *Cabaret*. The story is set in Berlin as the Nazis take over. The character who stayed with me was Herr Schultz, the Jewish fruit seller who was romancing the landlady. At the end of the play, as the American writer urged him to get out of Germany, he optimistically said he would stay. Even though he was a fictional character, I still wonder what happened to him. He haunts me because he was so sure everything was going to work out fine.

I put this together with scenes from the *Handmaid's Tale.* One seemingly normal day an office meeting is called and all the women are "let go." Their bank accounts are frozen. A new law bars them from owning property. One day, their rights are gone.

These are just two small scenes, but it is their specific "smallness" that most frightens me. One scene watching an optimistic romantic making a hopeful decision, and another scene where the world collapses so suddenly, taking everyone by surprise.

As I now acknowledge, particularly as a woman of color, the higher possibility that a racist mass murderer could shoot me at my local grocery store, I give these fictional scenes much more weight.

The fear is that the yellow warning light has been on for a long time, and could turn red at any second.

OUR DEMOCRACY DE-PENDS ON WHAT HAPPENS IN THE 2020 ELECTIONS

Right now, our democracy is being stolen from us in a comprehensive manner. Since 2017 this administration has decimated, broken, and fractured our rights and freedoms, as well as our moral standing in the world.

It feels dramatic to say, but because of the current occupant of the White House, the state of our union is crumbling beneath our feet, and our democracy is in deep trouble.

PART 1

MISSION & PLAN

★ ONE ★

EVERY VOTE MATTERS IN 2020

TO SAVE OUR DEMOCRACY we need to win big in the 2020 election. Since every vote matters, one of the most important things we can do is to get unwoke voters to vote, and to vote with us.

WE NEED TO WIN BIG

While it is human nature to want a big win to assure victory, in the case of 2020, there is more at stake. Because fences are turning into walls, winning in 2020 is more important than ever.

Meanwhile, there are several factors that could come into play. We have seen each of these factors impact elections, and an important defense against them is to win overwhelmingly.

The Electoral College Has a Bias

We saw Hillary Clinton win the popular vote by 2.8 million and still lose the Electoral College by 74 votes. Al Gore also won the popular vote but did not prevail in the Electoral College.

According to National Public Radio (NPR), because the winner of the Presidential race is determined by Electoral College votes, not the popular vote, "A candidate only needs to win the 11 states with the most electoral votes to hit 270." It is a very particular situation, but possible.

NPR went on to show that "...by our final math, in 2012 that could have meant winning the presidency with only around 23 percent of the popular vote."

Additionally, an unequal distribution of Electoral College votes creates an advantage for states with smaller populations. Fair Vote, The Center for Voting and Democracy outlines an example:

> ***"For instance, each individual vote in Wyoming counts nearly four times as much in the Electoral College as each individual vote in Texas. This is because Wyoming has three (3) electoral votes for a population of 532,668 citizens (as of 2008 Census Bureau estimates) and Texas has thirty-two (32) electoral votes for a population of almost 25 million. By dividing the population by electoral votes, we can see that Wyoming has one 'elector' for every 177,556 people and Texas has one 'elector' for***

> ***about every 715,499. The difference between these two states of 537,943 is the largest in the Electoral College."***

Overall, this works out as a bias against the Democrats. This is one reason why we need to win big!

Foreign Interference in Our Election

Foreign meddling in our election has many tentacles and a huge potential for trouble.

In a July 2019 House Judiciary Committee Hearing Republican Representative Will Hurd asked Former Special Counsel Robert Mueller about Russian inference:

> ***". . . did you think this was a single attempt by the Russians to get involved in our election, or did you find evidence to suggest they'll try to do this again?"***

Mueller answered emphatically:

> ***"It wasn't a single attempt. They are doing it as we sit here, and they expect to do it during the next campaign."***

Additionally, election interference from China and other countries appears to have been requested by Trump himself. The 2020 election is definitely a target of state-sponsored trolls, hackers, and corrupt players of all ilks.

So what will be helpful in this scenario: Winning big!

Gerrymandering

The Republicans have been actively re-drawing voting districts in their favor for years now.

As it states on Barack Obama's *All On The Line* mission statement "...there is a fundamental structural barrier that prevents progress: rigged electoral maps drawn with surgical precision by politicians to preserve their party's political power and silence the will of the people."

It takes time to right these wrongs, and many of these rigged voting maps will be used in the 2020 election. This partisan gerrymandering is one of the reasons why we need to not only win big at the presidential level, but also at the state and congressional levels.

Voter Suppression

Through the passage of voter ID laws, restrictions on early voting, the purging of voter rolls, the closing of polling venues, and/or the tightening of voting hours, the Republicans have actively benefited their candidates.

For instance, in the 2018 Georgia gubernatorial race, various voter suppression techniques, including a voter purge, made the Republican's victory suspect.

As stated on the *Why We Fight* page of fairfight.com: "Efforts to discourage and disenfranchise voters—in voter registration, ballot access, or counting of votes—have a catastrophic effect on our democracy. . . ."

The response to this issue includes supporting those who advocate for election reform . . . and winning big in 2020!

REPUBLICAN FRAMING IS ANOTHER REASON TO WIN BIG

The fact that the Republicans, and Trump himself, have been so adept at political framing makes framing a factor in why we need to be proactive in creating a big tidal wave of Democratic voters in 2020.

Case in point: Compare *Make America Great Again* with *I'm With Her*. You can see how his tagline helped Trump win the 2016 election.

Remember that each is framing the same core message: *Vote for me!*

MAKE AMERICA GREAT AGAIN

VS.

I'M WITH HER

Make America Great Again

- It is simple.
- Makes a speakable acronym—MAGA.
- Focuses on a valid worry for many people—that America is not great for them anymore.
- "Make" is an active verb.
- "America" is patriotic.
- "Great" is aspirational.
- "Again" plays off the powerful *good ol' days* that has resonance with Trump's target voter.
- Creates a tribe of those who want America to be great.
- The message and acronym (including font and colors used) works well on hats, t-shirts, etc.

I'm With Her

- Has a contraction, making it less crisp.
- Not a speakable acronym—IWH.

» By the end, it is not focused on the voters or their concerns, but instead on the candidate.

» "I'm" is focused on voter, but in a benign way, and "be" is not an active verb. Also, "I" is less inclusive than "We."

» "With" is not aspirational or interesting.

» "Her" puts the focus on Clinton.

» Any creation of tribe is based on Clinton at the center, not the voter.

» Similar to "I'm with Stupid" from the t-shirt world.

» Out of the context of a political rally, it does not make much sense.

Remember, both were framing "vote for me."

Another Example of Republican Framing: "Climate Change"

You all know the threat of global warming. In fact, it is a bigger threat than ever. Thanks to the Republicans, most of us, and the media and all Republicans, now refer to it as "climate change."

In 2014 the Report from the Yale Program on Climate Change Communication found that "the term 'global warming' is associated with greater public understanding, emotional engagement, and support for personal and national action than the term 'climate change.'"

The Republicans, who did not want to acknowledge the issue, made a concerted effort to increase the use of the term "climate change." It was a planned campaign because they understood the power of framing. They have succeeded.

Listen with your now finely-tuned ear to the news on this issue. Do you hear global warming at all? Are the forums or specials on TV news about global warming or climate change?

As an alternative, some climate activists are now using the terms "climate action" and "climate crisis." By using "climate" the term is still linked to "climate change," a term people already know. By replacing the word "change" with "action" or “crisis,” the urgency of the issue is highlighted. Since many studies show that the issue is of great urgency, I use the word “crisis” It is honest and evokes the necessary attention this issue deserves.

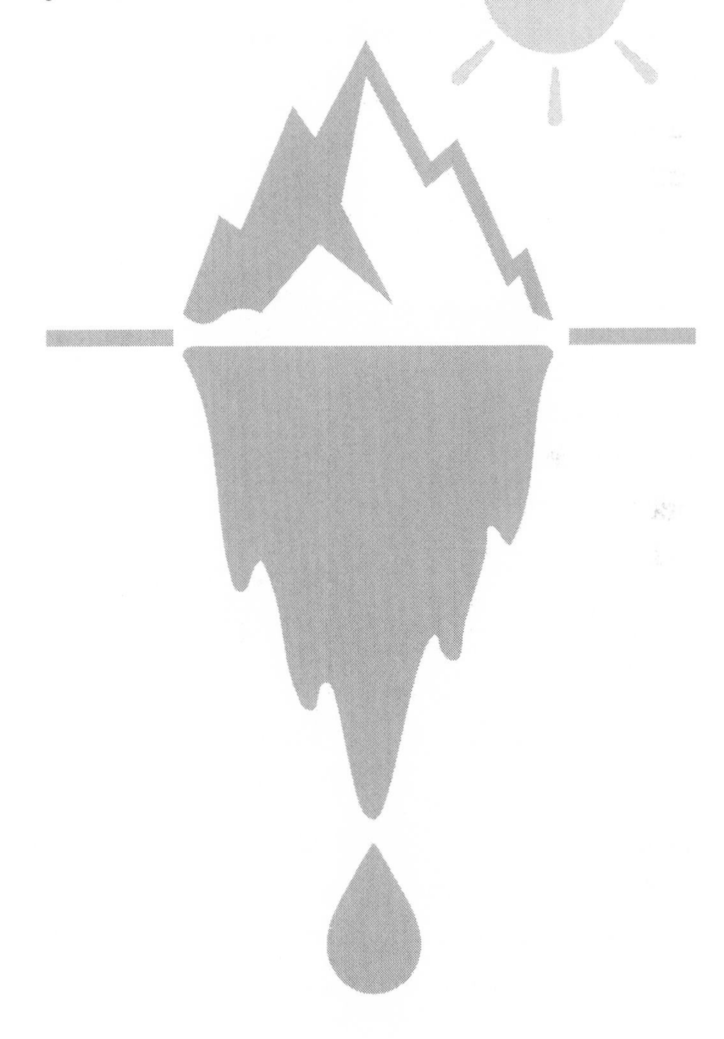

★ TWO ★

WAKE UP YOUR UNWOKE FRIENDS AND FAMILY

IF WE ARE GOING to win big in 2020, there are a whole lot of unwoke voters we need to tap into!

THE VOTING LANDSCAPE

There are four major voter groups:

1. Woke voters who are actively working to elect Democrats in 2020.
2. Woke voters who don't want Trump or his Republican enablers to win in 2020, but who are not actively involved in any political activities.
3. Unwoke voters who are undecided, apolitical, non-voting, and/or don't care about politics.
4. Unwoke voters who are Trump supporters and/or enablers, aka Trumplicans.

Hello Woke Voters

If you are a woke voter, either as an activist or not, this book is for you.

Your call to action is to wake up your unwoke, undecided, apolitical, non-voting, I-don't-care-about-politics friends and family.

As to your unwoke and entrenched Trumplican friends and family: They are still your friends/family and you need to honor that. But until the 2020 election is behind us, taking the time to reach *over the fence* to them might be time better spent in other ways.

But of course, if you see any opening, go for it. *Save Our Democracy* is about both winning the 2020 elections, and healing all the divides in our country.

YOU ARE THE BEST PERSON TO TALK TO YOUR FRIENDS AND FAMILY

You Are Perfect

No, this did not turn into a self help book! But who is better to talk to your unwoke friends and family than you? They already trust you, you have history together, and you see them in the normal course of your life. See, you don't even have to go out of your way to help save our democracy!

It is also more likely these friends and family would listen to you over a campaign worker, and many are not keeping up with current events, so don't even know the horrible things Trump and the Republicans are doing. Yes, you are the perfect one to talk to them!

Your Friends & Family Love You

Michelle is one of my best friends. We are close like sisters. So when Michelle saw me crying, she cared and asked what was up.

These days, I am less likely to mention a personal slight or heartbreak, and more likely to talk about news that has affected me. For instance, I told Michelle the story of a young refugee girl at the border. According to the news, her mother was taken away, which is bad enough. Then they took her doll, and I imagined them wrestling it from her arms. The tears on her face, her cries of confusion and fear, the shaking of her small body standing in a sea of uniformed legs and black boots, are the images that became real for me. I cried.

Because Michelle cares about me, she listened to the story. I felt like I took that little girl straight to Michelle's heart, and she could not look away. My unwoke friends are not uncaring, they just don't know what is going on in this time of Trump. By telling this story I framed it in a way that my friend could feel. She is generally unwoke and does not care about politics, but now she cares about that little girl.

Wherever You Go, There They Are

You don't have to be a candidate or campaign worker to talk to unwoke voters. They are already in your homes, neighborhoods, and communities—online and in person. One by one, as you go about your daily life, you can connect with your unwoke friends and family.

No extra mileage need be put on the car. Your time on social media does not have to be increased You don't have to give up bingeing TV shows or trying a new meal kit service. As you go about your daily life you already see and/or talk to them. You can choose to use your time with them in a *Save Our Democracy* way and you can do it in a way that does not even wake them up to the fact that they are getting woken up. If done well, it will just be a simple conversation with your friend or family member.

THE UNWOKE AMONG US

There are, of course, degrees of unwokeness. For instance, there are those who are undecided but not apolitical, or don't-care-about-politics but they vote. There are those who voted for Trump because they have always voted Republican and haven't thought any more about it since the election. I have many who lean over to me and "confess" that they voted for Trump, and will not again, but still don't care beyond their anti-Trump choice for the next election.

The biggest issue is that many of your unwoke friends and family do not realize that our country is not just on a slippery slope, but that the earth is crumbling right out from under us. They do not realize that we are in real danger as a democracy. They do not realize that if America's democracy falls, the whole world will fall.

They are often "swing voters" who don't take politics seriously, and don't understand that this is not politics as usual. They don't understand that we have to save our Democracy by getting Trump and his Trumplicans out of office in 2020.

THE MISSION

SAVE OUR DEMOCRACY

BY WAKING UP

Your Unwoke
Undecided
Apolitical
Non-Voting
I-Don't-Care-About-Politics

FRIENDS & FAMILY

THE PLAN BE-COME AN ALARM CLOCK FOR YOUR FRIENDS & FAMILY

At first, they will keep rolling over and using the snooze button, but with each ensuing conversation, you turn up the alarm volume just a bit. Finally, over time you will get them to actually wake up, and save our Democracy!

CONVERSATIONS CAN WAKE PEOPLE UP

Conversations can change the world. A good conversation changes minds, opens hearts, and establishes mutual understanding. Conversations can also be the perfect way to wake up your unwoke friends and family.

Conversation is an exchange of ideas, thoughts, feelings, etc. between two or more people. At its best, it is a mutual interaction, and as any communication can be, a conversation can be quite human and beautiful.

Unfortunately, in our culture, around political topics we end up in arguments or debates, or one person wants to lecture the other on what they believe the other person should believe. Real communication can easily get lost and shut down because all participants will rush to take a side and stand their ground. I imagine we have all been at holiday dinner parties where the communication shuts down in just such a scenario. This is no way to wake people up!

Conversations, on the other hand, can open dialogue and influence the people involved, but in a way that is respectful and authentic. When you see conversation as a way to reach out to people, to care in a sincere way, and yes, to wake people up to important truths, conversation can be a powerful alarm clock!

Pre-Existing Beliefs

As you have these conversations remember that many of your friends and family have quit listening to or watching any news, or worse yet, get all their news from Fox News, a Sinclair station, Trump News Channel, right-wing talk radio or their one-sided social media feed. The things they believe to be true will be greatly affected by this. Staying in conversation mode may be more difficult, but don't give in to the argument, debate, or lecture approach.

Conversation Seeds

Conversations by their very nature seem to move more slowly than debates or lectures. But in the long run, the seeds that can be planted in *over the fence* conversations can bear great fruit. Have a conversation and plant a seed. Have another conversation and water the seed...

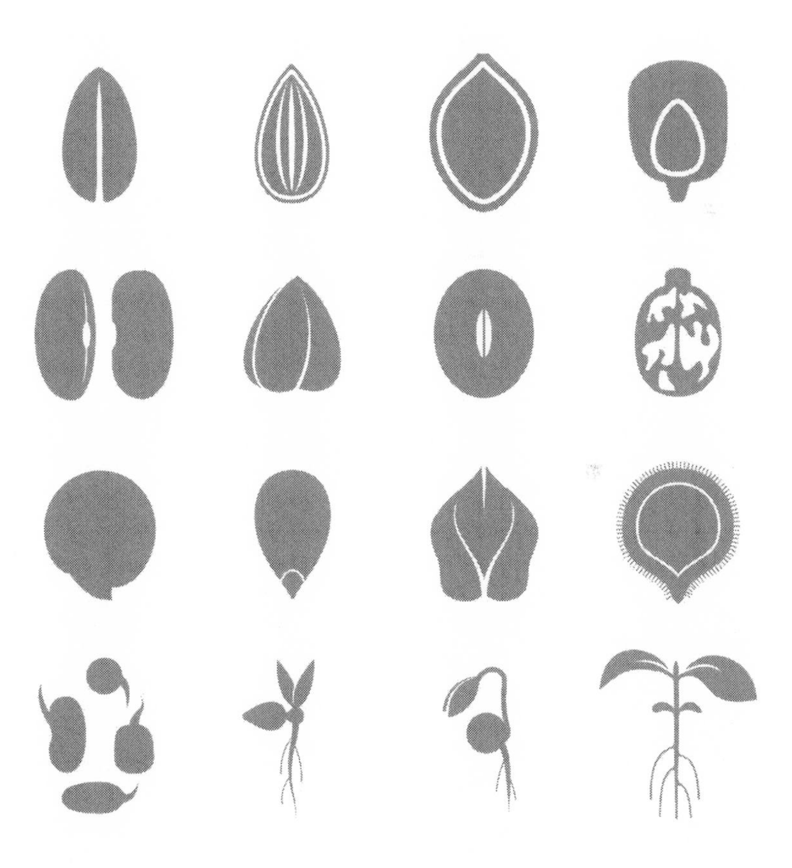

PART 2

STRATEGY

FRAME YOUR CONVERSATIONS

JUST LIKE FRAMING is used to superpower messaging on the national political level, you can use framing to next level your one-on-one communication with unwoke friends and family.

Framing changes the communication "map" by creating a way to have a "normal" conversation that includes politics. Framing will superpower your conversations with impact and influence.

FRAMING IS A SUPERPOWER

Framing is how you say what you say. It is important because the way you frame any given idea, opinion, thought, or even factual information, makes a large difference in how it is heard and received by your listener(s).

Framing is therefore a huge factor in how effectively you communicate your message, with the emphasis on how you influence, persuade, and move those with whom you are speaking.

On one hand, we are always framing. It's a natural part of communication. We are always making choices about how we say things. As example, how we talk to family members is different than how we talk to our bosses; and we choose our words carefully and consciously when talking to young kids or teenagers.

On a daily basis we are also the target of framing by advertisers. They use an arsenal of framing methods and various forms of media. Framing is a powerful tool of persuasion and a critical part of any sales transaction.

Of course, like so much of communication, framing is simple, and also quite complex and intricate. To help you frame your conversations, this section of the book lays out the three steps to framing your conversations and offers writing and practice exercises that will help you create your own framing for your own friends and family. This will superpower your *over the fence* conversations with them.

Most important is the fact that no matter how conscious you are about framing, it is impacting your life. In particular, it is a strong force in America's current political reality, a reality that is behind this *Save Our Democracy* call to action.

FRAMING IN POLITICS

Looking at how framing is used at the national political level is a good illustration of how framing works:

FRANK LUNTZ AND THE REPUBLICANS

The Republicans have had a "secret" weapon behind much of their success. Do you remember the 1994 "Contract With America"? It led to the Republican majority in the House of Representatives for the first time since the 1950s. Newt Gingrich is the politician who brought it to us, but Luntz's framing talent is behind the messaging.

Luntz calls himself a "language architect" and he certainly has a knack for building concise titles and phrases that have had a tremendous impact on our politics and policies. Just some of the Republican word choices he is behind:

» "Death tax" instead of "estate tax"

» "Illegal aliens" instead of "undocumented workers"

» "Exploring for energy" instead of "drilling for oil"

Death Tax. "Estate tax" sounds like a tax on the rich, which it is. By changing the messaging to "death tax" the Republicans built support against it. It is easy to feel overtaxed if you think you are even being taxed for your death. The target audience for this message includes citizens who already feel aggrieved about paying taxes at all.

Illegal Aliens. If you want to scare people about immigration, aren't "illegal aliens" more threatening than "undocumented workers"? Take a minute and visualize each of these labels. "Illegal aliens" sound scary!

Exploring for Energy. "Drilling for oil" sounds so invasive and uncomfortable, while "exploring for energy" sounds quite environmental and I imagine it being an adventure featured in *National Geographic!*

Lockstep Messaging

In this introduction to Frank Luntz, it must be pointed out that the Republican party does their part in activating their framing. When he speaks, they listen and execute. They stay in lockstep message mode, down to the exact words. This is important because the exact words used make a difference.

GEORGE LAKOFF AND THE DEMOCRATS

When you mention political framing, many people think of George Lakoff. As Professor Emeritus of Cognitive Science and Linguistics at University of California, Berkeley, and author of many books, his expertise on framing is deep and multi-layered.

Lakoff wisely advises the Democrats "to keep their messengers on message, and be able to craft that message . . . as a persuasive story about democracy and governance that voters want to hear, and support." Unfortunately, Democrats have not employed framing as an effective strategy in the ways that Republicans have.

Three Important Points

While I have learned a lot about framing from Lakoff, here are three things that may be specifically useful to you in framing for your friends and family:

Core Values. Framing is about more than the language used. It is about the core values that the language reflects. In political conversations, this plays out in the consistent differences in the values of Democrats/progressives and Republicans/conservatives. For instance, for conservatives, respect for authority carries a high value. Meanwhile, a common progressive value is fairness.

Knowing the core values of your friends and family will give you a heads up on how to frame for them. The values are the filters through which they see the world, and can give you insight into how to frame your wake-up conversations with them.

The Strict Father Family. One of the metaphors that frames conservative views is what Lakoff calls the "Strict Father Family." In this worldview, there is a moral hierarchy that justifies the dominance of certain groups over others. These can be private relationships of the father over the mother and children, or society-wide relationships such as the rich over the poor, Western culture over other cultures, whites over non-whites, etc.

You can see how a *Strict Father Family* model plays right into many conservative viewpoints. For instance, Trump's *America First* ideas are based on a hierarchy which places America on top of the world order. His pull-out of American troops from Syria in October 2019 was then sold to his supporters as an *America First* win, saving American money and reducing our involvement in the Middle East.

The *Strict Father Family* viewpoint may not even be a conscious belief for your friends and family members, but if recognized, you can more successfully frame your conversations in ways that will wake them up.

Negating Frames. For multiple reasons, we find ourselves wanting to fight back against framing we disagree with by arguing against it—but it doesn't work. In the 2016 election cycle, Lakoff reached out to

Clinton's campaign because he could not just watch as Trump wrapped the "Crooked Hillary" frame around and around her neck.

Lakoff urged the campaign to avoid repeating Trump's messages, even if trying to dispute them. Unfortunately, they could not help themselves. They even put out commercials repeating Trump's accusations and claims, hoping to show him for the liar he is. Inadvertently, they just reinforced his false claims. Trying to negate a frame can actually make it more potent because of the repetition factor.

In the end, I don't think there is any debate as to how effectively the Republicans framed Hillary as "Crooked Hillary."

With your friends and family, trying to dispute a frame they believe may just reinforce it. Even if the belief is false, you might be more effective talking about your position, and not repeating theirs.

TRUMP FRAMING

A quick unfortunate nod to Trump himself. He is a very persistent framer. In fact, it seems to be an instinctual ability for him.

Take for instance, his nicknaming. Most of us still remember that Jeb Bush, Republican Presidential candidate, is "low energy." I state this as if a fact because Trump so successfully stuck the description to Bush.

When Trump called another Republican Presidential candidate, Marco Rubio, "Little Marco," he insulted him on several levels. The nickname still haunts Rubio, layering in with the "fan-boy" taunts about Rubio's current "lap-dog" support of Trump.

These insulting nicknames carry a lot of punch to them. Trump repeated "Low Energy Jeb" and "Little Marco" again and again, and successfully framed both men, much to their detriment.

Save Our Democracy FRAM-ING

The *Save Our Democracy* definition of framing is "saying something in a way that will wake up our unwoke friends and family."

TWO PIECES OF THE FRAMING PUZZLE

As you have just read, there are many aspects to framing. We will focus on two pieces of the puzzle:

1. The content of what is said. This includes the wide range of language choices we make.
2. How the content is delivered. For instance, do you engage in your conversation with confidence and intention? Do you repeat key phrases in a way that makes them stick? Do you keep the tone conversational instead of confrontational?

FRAMING TAKES TIME

It would be unusual to have one earth-shattering conversation that totally wakes up your friend or family member to such a degree that they immediately volunteer to work on every Democratic campaign and climate crisis protest.

In more cases than not, this will be a process. In discussing how *over the fence* conversations work to wake up our friends and family, we used the analogy of planting and watering the *Save Our Democracy* seeds. Consider framing to be your fertilizer for the seeds you plant and be assured that they can, over time, grow into a full landscape.

In fact, you might even end up having an election day party in 2020, with all your newly-awakened friends and family wearing *I Voted Democratic!* stickers.

FRAMING EXERCISES

My background is in university-level teaching, and then professional coaching, so I love exercises! Exercises help you superpower your framing and conversational skills. You can use them for deeper insight and framing ideas, and to practice the process.

At first, doing these exercises may not make you feel like you are saving our democracy, but just wait until you start waking up all of those unwoke people with your new superpower. These exercises are the basic workout exercises you do before playing in the big game.

There are exercises presented as writing exercises, but they can also be verbal exercises, and can be a buddy or group activity. These exercises will increase your ability to frame during a conversation and give you a "library" of framing to use.

There are also practice exercises. It may seem silly to practice conversation, but you will be surprised at how helpful it can be, especially in learning to talk about what is to some, the taboo subject of politics.

Another benefit of these practice exercises is the stepping-into-another-person's-shoes aspect to the role playing. I truly hope that after we save our Democracy, we keep communicating in ways that will heal the divides that have been opened, and empathy will be a huge factor.

A Creative Approach

My graduate degree is in Creative Writing, so you can guess that I find "creativity" to be a sacred word—in life, and in *Save Our Democracy* work.

That said, approach the writing exercises with a playful open mind and let your writing flow in a stream of "I trust myself so much that I will just write down whatever comes to me at this given moment and see what happens!"

Don't let these exercises take a lot of time or energy. Keep a playful, creative approach going and allow your writing to lead you.

A Note About Skipping The Exercises

You might be tempted to skip the exercises and just go out and have conversations with your unwoke friends and family. I suggest that you will enjoy your conversations more if you do the exercises, because your skills will be superpowered.

I believe that these are not normal times. Our democracy is at great risk. The Trump presidency is flooding us with misinformation, crazy accusations, and distracting lies. A time like this calls for your strongest framing and conversational skills.

Furthermore, superpowering your framing and conversational skills is an overall win, helping you reach *over the fence* in both your personal and professional lives.

THREE STEPS TO THE WELL-FRAMED CONVER-SATION

Many people, whether they are woke or unwoke, do not talk politics with their friends and family, and therefore feel uncomfortable talking politics with anyone. So whether the chicken or the egg came first, many of us have some hesitation around this type of conversation.

As someone who likes to talk about politics but does not enjoy arguments or debates, I would generally avoid political topics with unwoke friends and family. It was not an ideal situation.

I needed my own alarm clock to ring. I came to recognize that our current political situation is an urgent and important matter and that I needed to offer myself in some way to the cause of saving our Democracy. Yes, *Save Our Democracy* is the title of this book, but more importantly, because it is in my heart, I see it as a mission that must be undertaken, a Resistance movement that I need to be part of.

I also quickly found out that if I start blurting out my concern about these things, especially with unwoke friends and family, their ears fold in, their eyes roll and/or we end up in a political argument.

I had to learn how to talk about politics, and found that using the well-framed conversations as my basic approach was effective. Not only did my relationships with my friends and family sustain, and actually even prosper, from the conversations, but I have seen with my own eyes that people are waking up. I believe that people are ready to wake up.

THREE STEPS

Conversations are most often spontaneous, so having three steps may feel awkward at first. But as with framing, having the best conversations will be best served by some skill building and practice. With practice these three steps will become fluid and natural to you.

The three steps to well-framed conversations are:

1. Attentive Listening
2. Relevant Content
3. Engaged Conversation

These three steps will superpower your ability to wake up your unwoke friends and family!

ATTEN-TIVE LISTEN-ING

WHY ARE SOME of your friends/family members unwoke to what is happening in our country today? Why do they hesitate to wake up? Why do some of them choose to not even vote?

Answering these questions and more for your unwoke friends and family is key to being able to have *over the fence* conversations with them. Understanding them as openly and deeply as you can will allow you to frame your conversations in ways that reach over the fence.

This makes *Attentive Listening* your first step, and includes literally listening to what they say, as well as reflecting upon what they say and what you already know about them.

Note that reflection both before and after your actual conversation can exponentially increase the benefits of *Attentive Listening*. To help you, exercises are included in this chapter.

At this level of listening, the bet is that you will discover new things about even your best friends and closest family members!

LISTENING IS A LOST ART

The idea that listening has become waiting-for-your-turn-to-talk is popular, both as practice and observation.

When people think about having a conversation, they often believe that the more they talk the more successful the conversation will be for them. With *Save Our Democracy* conversations you might assume that you have to talk a lot in order to wake up your friends and family. In most cases, the exact opposite is true.

VALUABLE INTEL

Listening itself is valuable and can give others the gift of feeling heard. For our purposes, we are definitely focusing on using listening as a way to collect intel for our framing.

On some level we collect intel every time we speak to someone. We want to bring as much depth and consciousness to our listening as possible because it can superpower our framing.

It was the realization that Frank Luntz was a pollster that focused me on listening. He is so good at his word-craft because he knows his audience.

You are lucky, because you start off with an advantage that Frank Luntz does not have. You already know something about the people you are looking to wake up. On the other hand, listening for more intel will be worthwhile.

There are three levels of intel that will be useful:

1. Personal and Individual
2. The Deeper Dive
3. Core Level Insights

PERSONAL AND INDIVIDUAL

Start with how this person chooses to present themselves in the world, and end up inside, looking at how this person thinks, feels, and creates their world. At this level you are answering the question, "Who is this person?"

EXERCISE 1
Getting to Know Them

Begin by thinking about your unwoke friend or family member. Keep this person in mind while completing these exercises.

You will want to respond to the prompts in this exercise without spending too much time thinking about your responses. Instead, answer quickly, with authority and confidence.

Don't hesitate to make up your responses. Pretend you know and trust your intuition.

These are prompts you might look to answer via your listening, but since these people will be friends and family, you may already know many of the answers.

These prompts are meant as guides through your reflection on this person and are not meant to be turned into questions you directly ask your friends and family.

Some prompts might seem odd or silly. Don't worry, just answer them. You will be surprised how much the silly questions power this exercise!

My unwoke friend/family member is: ____ years old

Their birthday is in: ____________________ (month)

For breakfast this morning, my friend/family member ate: ________________________________

My friend/family member laughs when: __________
____
____

Last night my friend/family member had a dream about: ____
____

My friend/family member is:
married / single / widowed / has a partner / in a long-term relationship / ?

My friend/family member drives a: ______________
____

My friend/family member's favorite car is: ________
____

My friend/family member's parents are:
alive / passed

My friend/family member has: __________________
children of the following ages: ________________

My friend/family member has: ____________ siblings
older: ______________ younger: ______________

My friend/family member always knows: _________
____

The first thing I notice about my friend/family member's appearance is: ____________________
____

My friend/family member is most confident about: ____________________
____

My friend/family member's health is: ____________________
____

My friend/family member cries when: ____________________
____

My friend/family member has a:
dog / cat / both / other

My friend/family member loses sleep over: ____________________
____

My friend/family member thinks politics are: ____________________
____

My friend/family member thinks Trump is: ____________________
____

Write 1–2 paragraphs about anything you learned about your unwoke friend/family member on a personal or political level.

Make a list of issues your unwoke friend/family member is interested in.

Considering what you have discovered about your friend/family member, write for five minutes about what they say or do when you start to talk about politics or the upcoming election. Knowing this will prepare you for the actual conversation.

EXERCISE 2
Getting to Know Them Better

My friend/family member's favorite way to relax is:

My friend/family member feels hopeful when:

Is your friend/family member:
an extrovert or introvert?

Where is your friend/family member most comfortable? (In nature, at home, at work . . .) Describe the scene with details.

Where will you most likely find your friend/family member on Sunday morning?

Describe your relationship with your friend/family member.

Write a letter/email to your friend/family member telling them what you admire and love about them.

Knowing what you now know about your friend/family member, write a letter/email to your friend/family member to ask them to wake up. Name at least three topics/issues that will interest them.

The next day, read the letter you wrote and highlight sentences, phrases, and words that will wake up your friend/family member.

(The letters in this exercise are not meant to actually be sent to your friend/family member.)

THE DEEPER DIVE

At the second level, the biggest question is a "why" question: "Why is this person still unwoke?" You can imagine how the answer to this question would be beyond valuable in framing a way to talk to this person.

EXERCISE 3
A Deeper Dive

Which descriptions listed below most fit your friend/family member:

- Unwoke
- Undecided
- Apolitical
- Non-voting
- Doesn't care about politics

Imagine telling someone why your friend is unwoke, undecided, apolitical, non-voting and/or doesn't care about politics. Write 1-2 paragraphs about what you said.

Did your friend/family member vote in 2016? 2018?

Do you know who they voted for? Was it an informed vote?

If your friend/family member voted for Trump in 2016, has your friend/family member told you why? Why do you think they voted for Trump?

Does your friend/family member believe that Trump is looking out for their best interests?

What does your friend/family member feel strongly about?

Does your friend/family member watch television news or listen to news radio?
If so, what channel(s)?
If not, why doesn't this person listen to any news?

Did your friend/family member have a happy childhood? If not, in what ways was this friend/family member traumatized as a child?

Has your friend/family member sought professional help to overcome traumas from their childhood?

Has your friend/family member been the victim of or witness to a crime? sexual harassment? discrimination? violence of any kind?

Has your friend/family member been a victim of or witness to racial discrimination?

What generation American is your friend/family member? If not of Native American ancestry, when did their family members immigrate to America?

Does your friend/family member have a job/career that they are happy with?

Why is this person still unwoke?

In dialogue form, write out a best-case-scenario *Save Our Democracy* conversation between you and your unwoke friend/family member.

CORE LEVEL INSIGHTS

At this deepest level, you may see things that your friends and family don't consciously acknowledge or see themselves. So as you get to this depth you must be careful about staying non-judgmental, and you must resist imposing your insights on your friends and family.

At this level you are looking at core values and basic world views. Easier said than done, but also possible. And just imagine how great your conversations can be if you understand the core values and beliefs of your loved ones and you have the ability to frame your conversations in ways that will truly engage and embrace those values and beliefs. I would call it win-win.

As quick example, imagine if a core value of your unwoke friend is loyalty. Looking at Trump through the lens of loyalty is not so good for Trump. His lack of loyalty to anyone but himself is so evident! Because loyalty is important to your friend, planting the seed of this issue and continuing to water it, will grow it into a well-rooted tree.

EXERCISE 4
Core Level Insights

Life Structures

Does your friend/family member have a supportive family/friend structure in place?

What role do they play in this structure?

Do they feel comfortable and competent in this role?

Identity

Does your friend/family member feel loved and supported?

Does your friend/family member feel grateful and lucky in life?

Does your friend/family member believe they are successful?

Does your friend/family member feel safe in their immediate surroundings? Do they feel safe in general?

Is your friend/family member compassionate and empathetic towards others?

How does your friend/family member handle their anger and frustration?

View of Success

If your friend/family member feels unsuccessful, what/who do they blame? If your friend/family member feels successful, what/who do they acknowledge for the success?

Does your friend/family member compare themselves to others?

Is success in work and life a competition or a journey for your friend/family member?

Religious/Spiritual Beliefs

Does your friend/family member belong to a religious or spiritual group? Are they active in the group?

Do the beliefs and practices of this group have an impact on your friend/family member's daily life? If so, describe the impact.

Values

List twelve values that are important to your friend/family member. For example:

- » Community
- » Discipline
- » Equality
- » Fairness
- » Generosity
- » Honor
- » Individuality
- » Justice
- » Power
- » Responsibility
- » Sustainability
- » Truth

Circle one value from the list you made.

Ask and answer three questions about how this value shows up in your friend/family member's life:

For example, using fairness as the value:

1. Does your friend/family member feel that they have been treated fairly in terms of
   - » equal access to job/career opportunities?
   - » equal access to economic opportunities?
   - » the workplace?

2. Does your friend/family member worry about things being fair:
   - » for others?
   - » in their community?
   - » in their country?
   - » in the world in general?

3. Does your friend/family member believe that:
   - » Democratic politicians are fair?
   - » Republicans politicians are fair?
   - » Trump is fair?

How does this value affect your friend/family member's view of politics in general and the 2020 election specifically?

Based on what you learned in this exercise:

- » Write 1–2 paragraphs about how your friend/family member lives this value.
- » Write a story that your friend/family member would tell to exemplify this value.

» Write 1–2 paragraphs about how Democrats exemplify this value in their policies and candidates.

» Write 1–2 paragraphs about how the value provides a way to have an *over the fence* conversation with your unwoke friend/family member.

EXERCISE 5
Practice Role Playing

Partner up.

Tell your partner, who will play the role of your friend/family member, about this person. If you have done the Reflection/Writing exercises, you can share your responses with your partner.

Role play the conversation with your partner as your friend/family member.

Reverse roles: You play the role of your unwoke friend/family member and your partner plays you.

Debrief the conversations.

Write a list of at least three things you learned about how to talk *over the fence* to your friend/family member.

Ask your partner to list at least three things they learned about your friend/family member.

USING THE IN-TEL

Once you learn and practice this process, it will feel quite natural. It is really just good communication broken down into specific steps, and the addition of some good framing.

The bonuses are that you get to improve your communication with friends and family, and it can be fun to have these *over the fence* conversations!

I will break down the use of the intel into two categories. These are the categories at the heart of a debate in the Democratic party: Does the Democratic Presidential Candidate win by making the election a referendum on Trump or by advocating for policies that people want? Ultimately, it is up to you to decide which path, or combination of paths, to present to your unwoke friend or family member, and framing can help with both approaches.

For instance, I have a friend who is a golfer, which I knew, but had not thought about in terms of Trump. But when the book by Rick Reilly, *Commander in Cheat: How Golf Explains Trump* came out, I realized I had a way to frame Trump as a cheater. My golfer friend, it turns out, is extremely offended by a golf cheater. To this day I open up our conversations with "Well, do you want to know what the Cheater-in-Chief did today?" And most of the time I am able to plant at least one more seed against Trump.

My friend voted for Trump in 2016, but seems less and less inclined to do so again. I do believe that the golf cheating bothers him and could affect his vote.

Now if you go with the issue/policy approach, the equation can be simple. As example, a mother of a special needs child is likely to be interested in policies and funding for special needs children.

Also note that the more specific your intel, the more you will be able to focus your framing in a way that she can hear. If your friend's child participates in the Special Olympics, Education Secretary Betsy DeVos' proposed $17.6 million cut from Special Olympics in 2020 might be the specific information you can frame.

That our personal experiences affect our political views is evident in Republican Frank Luntz's change of heart about global warming. When the Bush White House replaced "global warming" with "climate change" it was at Luntz's urging.

After Luntz almost lost his house to the Skirball fire in California, he came to a new conclusion about climate issues and urged a 2019 Senate committee, "to use the language that motivates the American people to action" on the climate crisis.

★ FIVE ★

RELEVANT CONTENT

YOU HAVE YOUR INTEL and now you are ready to prepare for your conversations. Preparing conversation content ahead of time serves two purposes:

1. It gives you a "library" of ready-to-use interestingly-framed content.
2. It allows you to practice the skill of creating such content. This ability

will make your *Save Our Democracy* conversations, more fun and successful.

Since you want your content to have an impact and be remembered beyond the conversation, this chapter will help you frame what you say with powerful word choices, memorable metaphors, and personal stories.

POWERFUL WORD CHOICES

"The difference between the almost right word and the right word is really a large matter— 'Tis the difference between the lightning bug and the lightning."

—MARK TWAIN

Words are complex and intriguing, and when you combine them into phrases or sentences, the intrigue factor increases. Here are some reasons why words are not simply words:

WORDS AND MEANING

Synonyms

Framer Frank Luntz, noticed that climate activists often talk about the "jobs" that will be created by new energy companies. He points out that "careers" is a better word choice. A job can connote something you have to do but don't enjoy, whereas a career is exciting and connotes success.

Clear, Concise, and Interesting

An example of word choice with some depth is the "Green New Deal." It is clear, concise, and interesting. Just three clear and concise words tell us so much and give flavor and framing to the ideas behind the phrase.

It is interesting because of its connection to the New Deal. The New Deal was a series of programs and protections enacted between 1933 and 1936. They were focused on relief, recovery, and reform, and are credited with helping America recover from the Great Depression. The New Deal is seen by many as a positive and progressive achievement and many of its programs are still with us today.

Meanwhile, even for those who do not pick up on the historical layer, the idea of a "new deal" just sounds good. Who doesn't want a "deal" and a "new deal" sounds even more attractive.

Additionally, "green" is a color often associated with the environmental movement, but even without that reference, green is a word that connotes growth, health, and prosperity.

EMOTIVE WORDS

Words have feelings. Well, the words themselves don't experience the feelings, but they are emotive and anyone who has written a love letter or condolence note understands this.

Just like people, some words are more emotive than others. I can feel the "slashing" of my benefits much more than the "reduction" of them.

Consider the Bush "tax cut," which the White House spun as "tax relief." The word "relief" feels good, while the word "cut" makes me uncomfortable, even though I technically want a tax cut. My brain knows that "cut" and "relief" are really the same thing, but it is relief that I want.

VISUAL WORDS

"Kids in cages." Can you see it? Three short words and yet the images flood my brain. When you can get people to "see" images through your words, you have framed well.

THE SOUND OF WORDS

Words are all about sound and music. Rhythm, rhyme, and alliteration (the matching of the consonant at the beginning of multiple words) are just some of the factors that can boost the effectiveness of your language through sound.

There is also the natural sound of words, and how the sound affects "meaning." For instance, say the word "smooth" out loud. Does it sound smooth? Now do the same with "whack." It sounds like itself!

Democrat and Democratic

Trump and the Republicans again provide a successful example of framing around sound: You might have noticed that Trump likes to say "Democrat Party" instead of the proper "Democratic Party" Republicans as far back as Senator Joseph McCarthy in the 1950's have used this as an insult to Democrats, but of course, Trump takes it to new levels.

"Democrat" is a noun. "Democratic" is an adjective. The sound of "Democrat Party" has a very different effect, because it is a more abrupt word that ends in "-rat." Meanwhile, "Democratic Party" has more elegance to it.

To his credit, George W. Bush used the incorrect version in his 2007 State of the Union address, but later offered a humorous apology to the Democrats: "I appreciate you inviting the head of the Republic Party."

EXERCISE 6
Powerful Word Choices

Choose an issue, topic, or politician.

Example: Gun Control.

Make a list of words or phrases about this issue, topic, or politician. Write whatever comes to you.

Don't judge or worry about making sense at this point.

> Example: Violence, Murder, Mass Murder, Kids, Blood, AR15, Trigger, Assault, Safety, Gun Shows, Arizona, Giffords, Active Shooter...

Choose three words and write a few sentences about how each of these words makes you feel.

> Example: Kids.
> Kids make me feel happy.
> Kids make me feel protective.
> Kids make me feel hopeful.

Choose three words and find rhyming words for each of them. There are rhyming dictionaries online. As with the previous step, don't judge or worry about making sense.

> Example: Active Shooter.
> troubleshooter, computer, sharp shooter, scooter looter, suitor, tutor, prosecutor.

Choose three words and find words that begin with the same consonant. There are alliteration generators online. And again, no judgments or worries about making sense.

> Example: Safety.
> sane, salad, sand, service, sanity, saddle, sea, sense, saturation, stereo, samba, shaker, safety.

At this point, you should have a gaggle of words!

Identify any words or feelings that your unwoke friend/family member would find interesting.

If no words or feeling would be interesting to your friend/family member, try another round or another issue, topic, or politician.

Once you have identified words or feeling that would be interesting to your unwoke friend/family member, write at least three sentences and/or word combinations using the words you generated.

Example:
Kids Deserve Safe Schools.
It's about gun safety, not gun control.
Sane gun safety laws makes sense.

MEMO-RABLE META-PHORS

AND SIMILES TOO

Donald Trump is a: ____________________
____
____
____

How you fill in the blank could create a metaphor. Technically, a metaphor compares one thing to another. Sometimes a metaphor compares a complex thing to one that is easier to understand. For instance, "life is a roller coaster." Or a metaphor can add emotional and/or visual elements that make the original thing more relatable. For example: "The storm is an angry beast."

Metaphors are not always literally true. "Raining cats and dogs" is not literally true—but speaks to a "bigger" truth. On the other hand, Congresswoman Ayanna Pressley (D-MA) uses a literal truth to create a metaphor when she acknowledges Trump as only the "occupant of the White House." This is a skillful, subtle metaphor.

As a result of their effectiveness, metaphors can make what you say more memorable and tell the truth in a more powerful way. You can easily see how metaphors can benefit your framing.

As with framing in general, some people have a natural ability with metaphors. Metaphor-making is also a skill you can superpower with practice, and lucky for you, there are exercises in this book that will help.

"BORROWING" METAPHORS

Poets and comedians both use metaphors and we can certainly learn about metaphors from them. In fact, beyond learning, we can "borrow" metaphors from them, with proper attribution, of course. When you are waking up your unwoke friends and family, I am sure people like Stephen Colbert, Seth Myers, or Jimmy Kimmel will not mind if you use one of their metaphors.

FILL IN THE BLANK

So let's look at some of the ways the blank line that we began with has been filled in:

» **Donald Trump is a cancer:**
"Let no one be mistaken Donald Trump's candidacy is a cancer on conservatism, and it must be clearly diagnosed, excised and discarded."

—Rick Perry, (in 2015) Republican, former candidate for President, and former Trump Secretary of Energy

» **Donald Trump is a Real Housewife:**
"@realDonaldTrump has his tagline!

it's official, he's a Real Housewife: 'I can't be doing so badly because I'm President and you're not.'"

—Andy Cohen, Bravo TV, Late Night Television Host

» **Donald Trump is a baby:** The Baby Trump Balloon that appears at many anti-Trump rallies is a "bigly" metaphor!

USING ALARM CLOCKS

So, can metaphors really help you wake up your friends and family? They might note how clever and witty you are getting, but will it move them politically? I will argue "Yes!"

Metaphors are not only memorable, they are sticky! If you had lectured your friend/family member on politics and why they should care, it is likely to have gone in one ear and out the other. But a good metaphor will stick and they could be thinking about it for days! They will probably still be laughing about the image that was conjured up in their head when you talked about Trump as a Real Housewife! They probably will start watching Andy Cohen's show. Trust the metaphor! It is almighty and powerful.

Stephen Miller Is a Gorilla

It is not easy to reveal that I was playing around with a metaphor exercise and came up with this pretty basic and possibly boring metaphor about Presidential Advisor Stephen Miller. But there is more to the story!

From this simple metaphor I wrote a fictional story about how he was not liked by the other gorillas when he was young! I wrote him as a wounded but revenge-focused gorilla.

When I told this to my wonderful but unwoke friend, she perked up. I was complaining about how uncreative I was feeling, and she, a therapist, was suddenly interested in Stephen Miller. So, of course, I went on: I told her about his role in all the immigration/refugee issues. I blamed the children in cages on him. She leaned in even more. She is now following both the immigration issue and various presidential advisors. She just needed to go through the door of psychology. My "open the door" line to her was "Stephen Miller is a gorilla." Go figure!

EXERCISE 7
Start a Metaphor Collection

"Everything in life is metaphor."

—HARUKI MURAKAMI

Metaphors are all around us. As mentioned earlier, comedians use them frequently. Having a collection of metaphors will be both useful and fun. So fire up a page/folder on your computer and start finding metaphors!

Hunting Ground. Of course the media will be a rich source of metaphors, but you might be surprised to see how your friends/family members use metaphors without even realizing they are metaphorizing.

Suggestion. Start a specific *Save Our Democracy* Metaphors page/folder.

EXERCISE 8
Make a Metaphor

The most important point about making metaphors is to understand that the more play in your process, the easier it will be to come up with interesting metaphors.

Make lists of the following topics:

- Animals: lions, tigers, bears
- Types of weather: rain, hurricanes
- Colors: red, blue, crimson, rust, lime green
- Smells: skunk, gasoline, body odor

- Types of sounds: banjo playing, cars crashing, wind in trees
- Textures: smooth, rough, soft
- Types of people: criminal, good samaritan, con man, mob boss
- Jobs
- Foods
- Tools
- Athletic Activities / Sports
- Trees
- Musical Instruments

Make the Metaphor:

Fill in the blank: Trump is a ____________

Choose a word from your lists.

Try not to think about making a perfect metaphor. Just try everything!

Remember that metaphors do not have to be true in terms of reality. In reality, Trump is not a selfish hyena. On the other hand, a metaphor becomes very powerful if it reveals a truth that is real and valid. For instance, Trump is selfish. Furthermore, hyenas are known to be quite opportunistic.

Choose the three metaphors that are most interesting to you and write 1–2 paragraphs about each one.

Choose one or more metaphors that you could use in your *over the fence* conversations with your unwoke friends and family.

PERSON-AL STO-RIES

THE POWER OF STORY

"Now, we only had one car, so sometimes my dad had to hitch-hike and walk long stretches during the 30 mile trip home from the shipyards. One rainy night, Mom got worried. We piled in the car and went out looking for him—and eventual-ly found Dad making his way along the road, soaked and shiv-ering in his shirtsleeves. When he got in the car, Mom asked if he'd left his coat at work. He ex-plained he'd given it to a home-less man he'd met on the high-way. When we asked why he'd

> ***given away his only jacket, Dad turned to us and said, "I knew when I left that man, he'd still be alone. But I could give him my coat, because I knew you were coming for me."***
>
> —Stacey Abrams' Democratic Response to President Donald Trump's State of the Union on February 5, 2019.

Abrams went on to connect her story to what she called "this uncommon grace of community."

> ***"Our power and strength as Americans lives in our hard work and our belief in more. My family understood first-hand that while success is not guaranteed, we live in a nation where opportunity is possible. But we do not succeed alone—in these United States, when times are tough, we can persevere because our friends and neighbors will come for us. Our first responders will come for us."***

It is out-and-out cliche of me to talk about the power of story. But as with many cliches, it is true. Story is powerful.

In fact, I was going to skip the inclusion of story, because it has become such a buzzword, but then I remembered Stacey Abrams' story about her father. I will be re-telling this story for the rest of my life, not just because it was a good story, but because of the way it touched something deep in me.

Story is powerful because of the way it connects us. At its best, there is something about the narrative form that captures our very human-ness. Stories can be aspirational, truth-telling, heart-opening, and soul stirring. They can be about characters we relate to or want to be. They can cover small victories or huge defeats, or anything at all. Ironically, stories make life real, and therefore, worthwhile.

No matter what it is about story, you can imagine how stories, especially personal stories, can help you wake up your unwoke friends and family. They are part of your superpower.

USING STORIES

The Me Too Movement as well as the recent response to the assaults on Roe v. Wade are perfect examples of how powerful the sharing of stories can be.

People who are unwoke often feel that politics don't affect them. Stories can show your friends and family how politics impact their daily lives.

EXCAVATING YOUR STORIES

You may think your stories are not "good enough." Maybe you did not suffer enough? You may think that your stories are boring. Stop that!

Your personal stories are an important part of your framing superpower. Don't forget, you are on a mission to wake up your unwoke friends and family. They might run from a political debate with you, but they might listen if you tell them a story about not getting a health issue checked because of your expensive co-pays, or how a young man was arrested in your neighborhood for being a violent white nationalist. These stories will matter to your friends and family because you matter to your friends and family.

Candidate Stories

In addition to Stacey Abrams' use of story in her speeches, there are various 2020 candidates who are using personal stories in very positive ways. Listen for them and see how they use their stories to frame their message.

Your Story Library

Once you learn to excavate your stories, you will find that your story library is much fuller than you realized, and you will want to share the stories, especially in the service of saving our Democracy.

SHARING OTHER PEOPLE'S STORIES

When another person's personal story impacts you, you can tell the story of how you were impacted, and include the story itself. This can include the stories you hear through social media, books, television, radio, etc. This expands your story library and circulates stories that need to be told.

The Sandra Bland Story

Sandra Bland was a 28-year-old African-American woman who was pulled over for a minor traffic offense as she drove through Waller County, Texas. The arresting officer, who had a history of pretextual traffic stops, escalated the situation (as seen on video evidence), resulting in Bland's arrest. She was held in county jail for three days before she was found hanged in her cell. Her death was ruled a suicide, but to many, both her arrest and death are still suspicious and unsolved.

Stories like Bland's need to be told, but some of your friends and family may feel uncomfortable about discussing social justice issues, which means you may need to find ways to make the stories personal.

This story impacts me on several levels. First of all, it would cause any citizen to worry about being pulled over by a cop looking to find trouble. Unfortunately, this fear is even more pressing for people of color. As a woman of color, Bland's story makes me feel vulnerable.

Bland's story also impacts me because I can feel her anger and fear at being put into such a distressing situation, from the escalation of the traffic stop, to being held in a solitary cell for three days.

Finally, Bland's story impacts me because of the injustice I feel about her death. This did not happen in the 1950's. This happened in July 2015.

When I was considering a cross country drive by myself, I was able to "insert" this story when talking to friends about my trip. I believe I planted an important seed in those conversations.

TELLING STORIES

Some tell stories by listing "what happened." The storyteller can see and feel the story, but only tells you the basic plot, and you are left with a rather dry storyline. But a story can be so much more. At its best, a story can transport the reader into its reality. It is, then, the perfect vehicle for waking up the unwoke.

Notes about Stories

There are some common elements to stories that will help you bring them alive for your unwoke friends and family:

Know your audience. In the case of your *Save Our Democracy* stories, your audience is built-in—your unwoke friends and family.

Something happens. In a story, there is some transformation that occurs, most often to the main character.

The six-year-old refugee was tired and scared, but her parents were taking care of her. Once they crossed the U.S. border, she was taken away from them. At the end of the story she is alone. Everything changed dramatically for her and her family.

Know your core theme. In Star Wars, the core theme is good against evil. What idea are you choosing to promote in your story? How will it frame your conversation?

Create a hook. Add something to your story that will capture the attention of your friend/family member. Use your intel and previous knowledge and create your hook based on what interests them.

If you are telling the story about the young girl taken from her parents at the border to someone who has a young child, you might create a story hook around that person being a parent: "The young mother had to be dragged away by three large Border Patrol officers when she realized what was going to happen. Only after the door was slammed shut did she stop fighting."

You can make the hook even more potent by adding a conversation hook: "I'm sure that as a parent, you can only imagine how horrible it would be to have your child taken from you."

Bring your reader into the story. You want your listener(s) to feel like they are there, in the scene of the story, so set the scene—use all five senses and immerse your friends and family into the story. Let them "experience" the characters, setting, and action of the story.

EXERCISE 9
Excavate Your Stories

Many of us have a few go-to personal stories, often revolving around a lesson we learned or good times we had. We also have a treasure trove of stories that do not come to mind easily. If you want to excavate more stories, this simple technique can help pull up more memories.

Create a document/page with the following sections:

0–10 years

10–20 years

20–30 years

30–40 years

Of course, add decades as needed.

Start filling in stories. Write a quick note as reference so that you will remember the story later.

The most difficult part of this exercise is getting the ball rolling. Stay with it!

Once you start this exercise, it may continue on its own while you are doing other things, so you might want to keep your smart phone or some paper and a pen nearby.

EXERCISE 10
Movie Loop

This exercise will help you expand your story telling skills beyond "and then this happened." The goal of the exercise is to open up the idea of creating a scene instead of just listing the plot points. Enjoy!

Use an existing story or write the first draft of a new one.

Outline the story as written.

Choose a scene from the story.

Take note of the setting, the characters, and the action.

Close your eyes and watch the scene as if it is a scene in a film.

Take notes about what you noticed about the scene.

Put the scene on "loop" and watch it at least seven times.

Take notes about what you notice each time you watch.

Write the scene.

> Note: You will not use all the things you noticed, but you now have some specifics details that you can include. Specific details can both ground and heighten a story.

RELE-VANCE IS KEY

RELEVANCE IS THE FINAL FACTOR

Word choice, metaphors, and stories can help you create content that is clear, concise, and interesting, but your final framing goal is relevance, specifically the relevance your framing has with your unwoke friends and family. *Relevant Content* will make your *over the fence* conversations powerful and effective.

Personal Experience is the Filter

It comes down to this: Your personal experience affects what feels relevant to you. So when considering how to wake up your friends and family, looking through the filter of their experiences will be a large factor in the content you choose to share with them.

Sharing the legal and historical aspects of impeachment may not provide a wake up call to your friend/family member who is busy getting three kids ready to start a new school year, but this same friend might be interested in hearing about issues of gun safety. That the Republican-controlled Senate is blocking a background checks bill passed by the House might be very relevant.

Talking about the tragic situation in Syria may not wake up your friend/family member who was just diagnosed with a health issue. But approached from another angle, this person who is understandably feeling like life is unfair, could be woken up by the basic issue of unfairness, in that America is abandoning an ally. And of course, health care and health insurance are topics that might be relevant to this friend/family member.

The Editing Room Floor

Using the filter of relevance means that some of your best word choices, metaphors, and stories may go unused. Just like a great movie editor leaves many excellent scenes on the editing room floor, your discipline in staying relevant is most important.

Proactive Relevance

Trump brags about cutting "government regulations" because he has already framed "regulations" as harmful to his supporters. He has proactively created relevance for his base by giving "regulations" a negative connotation.

George Lakoff points out that you can call government guidelines and rules "regulations" or "protections."

So what if the Democrats adopted "protections" instead of "regulations?" In fact, it could be argued that a "protection" is a more accurate description of a government guideline or rule.

Since a government protection is something that can be framed as relevant to anyone, it could be especially effective to talk about how Trump is cutting so many "government protections" when you are waking up your unwoke friends and family.

EXERCISE 11
Relevance

In looking at the framing you have created, or are "borrowing" from others, choose framing that will be particularly relevant to the unwoke friend/ family member you are ready to wake up.

Take a few minutes before your conversation to write down the words, metaphors, and/or stories you want to use in your conversation.

List the ways that these words, metaphors, and/ or stories will be relevant to your friend/family member.

Imagine the conversation and take some notes about how it goes.

Be grateful for this opportunity to save our Democracy! Go forth and engage!

EN-GAGED CONVER-SATION

THERE IS A SCENARIO where you walk into a room and immediately get the rolled-eyes-and-walk-away response from your unwoke friends and family. In this situation, where there used to be fences, there are walls.

But there is another vision: Your friends and family are glad to see you. You have found ways to inject well-framed messages instead of "politics" into your conversations. In fact, some of them have already woken up, and you can see the seeds sprouting in others. Your friends Dan and Lynne are still Trumplicans, but now you actually share Trump jokes with them.

Your *Save Our Democracy* work makes this vision possible. It is because you did the prep work of *Attentive Listening* and *Relevant Content*, and then you engaged in conversations in ways that opened doors instead of slamming them in anger. Engagement works. Conversations work.

You are saving our Democracy, one friend or family member at a time!

GETTING TO IT

On one hand, you can start waking up your unwoke friends and family while going about your days as usual. You are still going to that family dinner, still meeting that friend for lunch. Yet each seemingly casual conversation is part of your *Save Our Democracy* work.

You can add a concerted effort to reach out by identifying the unwoke people in your life, or being consciously open to meeting them as you go about your life.

Remember, with each person, this is a process—one step at a time. Remember the planting metaphor, one seed and some water is the first step, then more water, then a sprout, and in the end, and in time for the 2020 election, a mighty tree or blossoming flower. Whatever your preferred metaphor, our Democracy is better off for it.

So be patient, and keep talking!

ENGAGEMENT FACTORS

There are several factors to consider in delivering your *Save Our Democracy* conversations:

- » Speak intentionally
- » Focus on the relevant
- » Ask questions

- » Stay in conversation mode
- » Use repetition

SPEAK INTENTIONALLY

The more confident you are about your framing, the easier it will be to speak from a place of intention. When I know I have framed what I am saying and that what I say will be influential, I can speak without anxiety or anger and in a way that is kind and helpful, honest and authentic. And instead of backing my unwoke friend or family member into a corner, I can allow space for true conversation.

FOCUS ON THE RELEVANT

The most important element in superpower framing is what the swing voter hears. It is not enough to come up with some brilliant creative spot-on framing that you love. It is not enough to come up with a brilliant argument to show off what you know and why you are right. It is all about what that friend/family member hears. It is about how relevant the framing is to the person you are talking to.

ASK QUESTIONS

Questions not only help you collect more intel about your friend/family member, but they keep the person engaged in the conversation. You show that you are listening to them, which will more fully open them up to the conversation. Two wins in one!

Additionally, asking a question instead of finding fault or disagreement may be exponentially more effective. For example, instead of accusing them of being wrong or misinformed about issues such as women's reproductive health or LGBTQ rights, ask your friend/family member about their viewpoint, and see if you can get to some of the "why" behind that viewpoint. If you ask questions to draw out conversation, then listen, your friend/family member might just listen to your thoughts on those issues.

STAY IN CONVERSATION MODE

Heather McGhee, an African-American, who is currently a Distinguished Senior Fellow at Demos, a progressive think tank, was on C-SPAN when a man called in and said he was a racist. To his credit, he added that he did not want to be one.

Much to McGhee's credit, she did not react with name-calling or hate. She did not lecture him for being wrong. Instead, she chose to have a conversation with him... and she spoke in a way that he could hear. She began her response:

> ***"Thank you so much for being honest and for opening up this conversation, because it is simply one of the most important ones we have to have in this country."***

She went on to say:

> ***"...so your ability to just say 'this is what I have, I have these fears and prejudices, and I want to get over them,' is one of the most powerful things that we can do right now at this moment in our history."***

Their conversation has continued to this day, and includes them meeting in person.

His views of black people have changed dramatically, and McGhee and this man are now friends. It is amazing what well-framed conversations can do.

USE REPETITION

Repeating key words (or in Trump's case, nicknames, insults, and lies) is key. One of the reasons the Republicans have been so proficient at framing is that they are disciplined at lockstep messaging. They turn repetition of key words into a lethal weapon. Reagan, George W. Bush, and now Trump, are all good at sticking to the message, over and over again.

Example: "Fake News"

One of Trump's favorite phrases is "fake news." He loves to throw this phrase at the collected media or use it to rile up his base supporters. You can't be an American and not know that Trump thinks the news is fake—or does he?

In an on-stage conversation with *PBS News*' Judy Woodruff, *60 Minutes* correspondent Leslie Stahl said:

"It's just me, my boss, and him—he has a huge office—and he's attacking the press. There were no cameras, there was nothing going on and I said, 'That is getting tired, why are you doing it? You're doing it over and over and it's boring. It's time to end that, you've won the nomination. And why do you keep hammering at this?'

And he said: 'You know why I do it? I do it to discredit you all and demean you all so when you write negative stories about me no one will believe you.'

So, put that in your head for a minute."

EXERCISE 12
Engaged Conversation

Conversation Notes

You might want to jot down some notes both before and after your *Save Our Democracy* conversations.

The notes before the conversation will help you more successfully talk over the fence, and the notes taken after will both allow you reflection and help you prepare for your next conversation with this unwoke friend/family member.

EXERCISE 13
Practice Role Playing

As in so many things, the best practice is in the doing. But let's not assume that practicing these conversations is silly. Role playing with a partner, or even into a mirror, will help you feel more comfortable about your conversations.

Remember, most of us never received instructions on how to talk about politics with others, especially with those who are unwoke.

PART 3

TAKE ACTION

MADA

MAKE AMERICA DEMOCRATIC AGAIN

WE ARE HOPEFUL that all Democratic candidates across the United States get their framing together, and provide the kind of strong messaging that wakes up our unwoke friends and family. Meanwhile, let's all do the "advance work" and talk *over the fence* to the unwoke people in our lives. Let's start saving our Democracy right now!

At this point, you have superpowered your ability to talk about "politics" with your unwoke friends and family. If you have followed along, you have some well-framed messages in your *Save Our Democracy* library, and the skill of framing, that you can use on-the-fly during any conversation. Your *Attentive Listening* has added to your understanding of what is relevant for your friends and family. Finally, if you did the practice exercises you have some experience under your wings.

So finding ways to bring up *Save Our Democracy* topics in your conversations should feel natural. Very quickly you will find yourself looking forward to the opportunity to have well-framed conversations.

HAVE A PLAN

If this book just made you more conscious of your unwoke friends and family, or planted a few seeds in you to consider talking politics with some of your friends, great!

Honestly, I hope the seeds got planted in Chapter One and have grown into at least a medium-sized tree by now. For you, a plan:

Prepare

» ID the unwoke friends and family you are going to wake up. Suggestion: Start with three. If you only focus on one person, you might be disappointed if the process is slow and if you focus on too many people, it will be more difficult to master your new superpower.

» Do the exercises. Don't skip the Role Playing!

Create the Habit

» Remember that a conversation a day keeps the Authoritarian Fascists away.

ENLIST OTHER WOKE PEOPLE

With your *Save Our Democracy* conversations you are enlisting unwoke friends and family to vote and maybe even participate in the 2020 election. There is one more group you can influence: Your fellow woke citizens. No matter what else they are doing, they can add *over the fence* conversations to their daily lives. We can indeed become a *Saving Our Democracy* tidal wave.

Recruiting others to join you in this work will also give you practice buddies or groups.

TALK TO FRIENDLY STRANGERS

Waking up unwoke *friendly strangers* along the way can be very rewarding. Every errand or waiting room is an opportunity to have a *Save Our Democracy* conversation with someone.

Your initial reaction might be to shy away from this, but let me remind you that you have a mission, plan, and strategy, and you have sharpened your framing skills by reading this book. So you just might find yourself talking to someone in the grocery store line. In many cases, they will welcome the conversation. There is no reason for you to be shy, because you are on a *Save Our Democracy* mission!

With *friendly strangers* you will not have time to sit down and reflect, but if you have already done some of the exercises and have trained yourself to be an extraordinary listener, you will surprise yourself with how much you can discern about *friendly strangers*. Even the way someone says "Trump" can tell you a lot.

So use your superpower and talk to them!

BEYOND THE CONVERSATION

While this book has focused on the one-on-one interaction with one unwoke friend/family member at a time, you can also use your *Save Our Democracy* abilities to speak up in many other ways:

» Public speaking in informal and formal situations

» Posting on social media

» Communication with your elected officials

» Letters to the Editor, opinion pieces

» Blog posts, or articles

» In songs, art, videos, or podcasts

Additionally, if you are interested in working for campaigns, but hesitant to be a canvasser, this training in well-framed conversations will help you feel more confident about talking to other voters, including *friendly strangers.*

Remember, many of us never learned how to talk about politics with others. With *Save Our Democracy* conversations you will learn to be more articulate and engaging—about political topics, and in general.

MEASURING SUCCESS

You might think you are getting nowhere, only to find out a week after the election that someone you have been trying to wake up, did indeed wake up and go to the polls. This person might even cast "blame" and say they only went because of you, and you can just smile at that. And yes, they voted Democratic, and yes they took a friend, who voted too. I would count this as a success!

With seed planting we just can't tell when a seed is going to break open and prosper. And we also realize that some seeds may be forever dormant, until they are not.

Our Democratic tidal wave in 2020 will be measurable, but on the individual basis, success can be more difficult. So measuring success is best placed in your own improved communication and framing skills, and improved relationships with your newly woke or even still unwoke friends and family.

SEVENTH GENERATION PRINCIPLE

On the other end of the measurement scale is the Seventh Generation Principle. According to this principle, with roots in indigenous philosophy, you should consider the consequences of your choices seven generations into the future when making decisions in the present.

In the saving of our Democracy, where will you stand? What legacy will you leave to your children, grandchildren, and beyond?

KEEP TALKING

Ultimately, the biggest measure of *Save Our Democracy* success will be you continuing to talk to your unwoke friends and family, and continuing to find ways to reach them by framing the conversation for them.

As final reminder, your call-to-action for *Save Our Democracy* is:

» Focus on waking up **your unwoke friends and family.**

» Talk to them **over the fence** using well-framed conversations.

» Create a **tidal wave** of Democratic voters in 2020 and . . . .

MAKE AMERI-CA DEM-OCRATIC AGAIN!

NOTES

Chapter One

1. Kurtzleben, Danielle. "How To Win The Presidency With 23 Percent Of The Popular Vote." NPR. November 2, 2016. Accessed November 1, 2019. https://www.npr.org/2016/11/02/500112248/how-to-win-the-presidency-with-27-percent-of-the-popular-vote.

2. "Problems with the Electoral College." FairVote: The Center for Voting and Democracy. Accessed November 1, 2019. https://archive3.fairvote.org/reforms/national-popular-vote/the-electoral-college/problems-with-the-electoral-college.

3. "Full transcript: Mueller Testimony Before House Judiciary, Intelligence Committees." NBC News. July 25, 2019, 8:45 AM PDT / Updated July 25, 2019, 8:58 AM PDT. Accessed November 1, 2019. https://www.nbcnews.com/politics/congress/full-transcript-robert-mueller-house-committee-testimony-n1033216.

4. "One Person. One Vote." All On The Line. Accessed November 1, 2019. https://allontheline.org/#mission.

5. "Why We Fight." Fair Fight. Accessed November 1, 2019. https://fairfight.com/why-we-fight.

6. "What's In A Name? Global Warming vs Climate Change" Yale Program on Climate Change Communication. May 27, 2014. Accessed November 1, 2019. https://climatecommunication.yale.edu/publications/whats-in-a-name-global-warming-vs-climate-change.

Chapter Three

1. Dr. Frank Luntz, Words That Work: It's Not What You Say, It's What People Hear (New York: Hachette Books, 2007)

2. Morrison, Patt. "Column: Linguist George Lakoff on What Democrats Don't Understand—and Republicans Do—About How Voters Think." Los Angeles Times. November 28, 2018. Accessed November 1, 2019. https://www.latimes.com/opinion/op-ed/la-ol-patt-morrison-george-lakoff-20181128-htmlstory.html

3. George Lakoff, The All New Don't Think of an Elephant!: Know Your Values and Frame the Debate (White River Junction, Vermont: Chelsea Green Publishing, 2014)

4. Rathje, Steve. "The Power of Framing: It's Not What You Say, It's How You Say It." The Guardian. July 20, 2017 05.18 EDT Last modified on July 5, 2018 16.49 EDT. Accessed November 1,

2019. https://www.theguardian.com/science/head-quarters/2017/jul/20/the-power-of-framing-its-not-what-you-say-its-how-you-say-it.

Chapter Four

1. "Testimony of Dr. Frank I. Luntz Senate Democrats' Special Committee on the Climate Crisis July 25, 2019." Brian Schatz United States Senator for Hawai'i. July 25, 2019. Accessed November 1, 2019. https://www.schatz.senate.gov/imo/media/doc/Frank%20Luntz%20Testimony.pdf.

Chapter Five

1. Yoder, Kate. "Frank Luntz, the GOP's message master, calls for climate action." Grist. July 25, 2019. Accessed November 1, 2019. https://grist.org/article/the-gops-most-famous-messaging-strategist-calls-for-climate-action

2. Hobson, Jeremy. "You May Have Heard Republicans Use The Term 'Democrat Party.'" Here & Now. February 07, 2019. Accessed November 1, 2019. https://www.wbur.org/hereandnow/2019/02/07/why-republicans-say-democrat-party

3. Blake, Aaron. "The Many Metaphors for Donald Trump." The Washington Post. May 7, 2017. Accessed November 1, 2019. https://www.washingtonpost.com/news/the-fix/wp/2017/05/07/the-many-metaphors-that-describe-donald-trump.

4. Ibid.

5. "Full text of Stacey Abrams' Response to Trump's State of the Union" NBC News. Feb. 6, 2019. Accessed November 1, 2019. https://www.nbcnews.com/politics/congress/full-text-stacey-abrams-response-trump-s-state-union-n968221

6. White, Daphne. "Berkeley Author George Lakoff Says, 'Don't Underestimate Trump.'" Berkeleyside. May 2, 2017, 3 p.m. Accessed November 1, 2019. https://www.berkeleyside.com/2017/05/02/berkeley-author-george-lakoff-says-dont-underestimate-trump

Chapter Six

1. "Clip of Progressive Issues in Campaign 2016 Garry from North Carolina talks to Heather McGhee." C-SPAN | Washington Journal. August 18, 2016. Accessed November 1, 2019. YouTube video. https://www.c-span.org/video/?c4685742/garry-north-carolina-talks-heather-mcghee.

2. "Deadline Club Awards 2018 Dinner Conversation with Judy Woodruff and Lesley Stahl." Deadline Club. May 22, 2018. Accessed November 1, 2019. YouTube video. https://www.youtube.com/watch?v=nq6Tt--uAfs

GRATI-TUDE

I WAS BLESSED with two editors who are close readers, in-depth thinkers, and woke Americans! I am deeply grateful to Elgee Tavanlar Amato and Gayle Sato.

This book came alive because of the design work of Susan Shankin. I am so appreciative of the interior "landscape" that Susan gave me to work with. I felt like my text was literally drawn out by the design.

Additionally, thank you to Dede Moore, who would do spot readings and edits that kept me writing. Dede is also behind my introduction to many activist groups, several of whom invited me to speak.

Scott Bowman was a valued guide and mentor as I found my path with *Save Our Democracy*. In fact, I found this trailhead because of the scope of his insight and the power of his coaching. Scott is the very definition of a coach—at the highest level.

Through the deep and healing work of Denise Warner, I feel able to mission-ize *Save Our Democracy*, and I am grateful to be powered up in this way.

As well, I want to acknowledge the many groups and individuals who hosted events and invited me to speak. And to my Facebook friends who consistently supported *Save Our Democracy* posts, especially in its early days, when it was *Talking Over The Fence*. Your support was crucial and valuable to this book.

To my soul-sister-friend Victoria Almeida. She is the one who took me to see Cabaret in 2016. She died in December of 2017, but has been with me as I wrote this.

Finally, to the friends and family who are my gold *kintsugi*. I bow deeply in gratitude.

ABOUT

SAKADA

SAKADA IS A NERDY poet/writer who loves to play with words, metaphors, and stories. Sakada has committed herself to helping woke people create well-framed political conversations that will wake up their friends and family to vote Democratic in 2020.

Her degrees are in Journalism (University of Michigan-BA) and Creative Writing (Antioch-MFA). As full time university faculty, Sakada taught at both undergraduate and graduate levels. She works with private clients as a ghostwriter and writing/book consultant. She is available as a speaker and consultant for *Save Our Democracy* and political message framing in general. She also offers *Save Our Democracy* workshops and "think tanks."

ABOUT

SAVE OUR DEMOCRACY

Stay in Touch

SaveOurDemocracyBook.com
SaveOurDemocracyBook@gmail.com

---

fb.me/Sakada.SaveOurDemocracy
twitter.com/_save_democracy
instagram.com/_saveourdemocracy

Speaker

Sakada is available to speak on *Save Our Democracy*, and framing in general.

Consultant

Because *Save Our Democracy* work is useful to advocacy groups and campaigns, Sakada serves as a consultant to advocates, canvassers, and candidates on various *Save Our Democracy* topics, from communication/conversation training to message/issue framing.

Training—Online or In Person

Workshops

For groups who want hands-on training in *Save Our Democracy* conversations. The workshops are designed to fit the needs of your group.

"Think Tanks"

For groups who want to dive in and "think tank" an issue or candidate. Gather your best colleagues and fellow advocates together and over a series of three sessions we will create impactful messages that are true to your group's mission. These sessions are designed to fit the needs of your group.

Made in the USA
Columbia, SC
23 December 2019

85573971R00086